Pauline Dohmen

Mein Klimperklein PROJEKTBUCH

Gestalten, Planen und Ausmalen

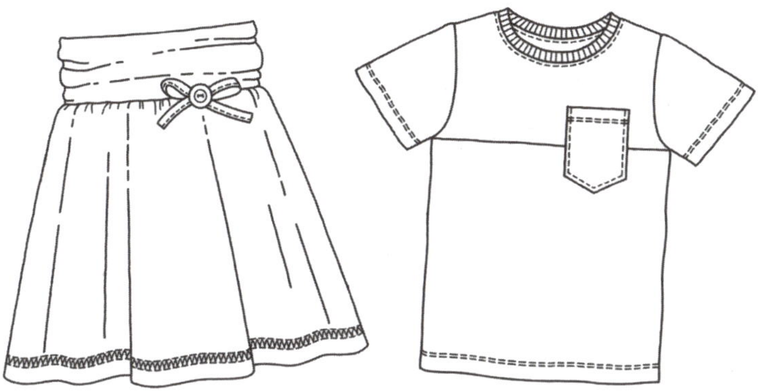

INHALT

20 Modelle

Liebe DesignerIn,

mit diesem Projektbuch konnte ich mir einen kleinen Traum erfüllen: Ein richtiges klimperkleines Mal- und Designbuch. Als ich ein kleines Mädchen war, haben wir zu Hause oft „Schneiderei" gespielt. Zeichnerisch habe ich die meist extravaganten „Bestellungen" meiner Mama oder Oma umgesetzt und festgehalten. Mit diesem Projektblock ist mein Spiel nun erwachsen geworden.

Ob Erwachsener oder Kind, jeder kann mit diesem Buch zum Designer werden und auf Basis meiner Schnittmuster ganze Kollektionen konzipieren und planen.

Zeichne Muster, Applikationen, Farben und Verzierungen, klebe Stoffproben ein und notiere alle wichtigen Informationen. So wird schon die Planung des genähten Kleidungsstücks zum kreativen Vergnügen!

Ich hoffe, du hast genau so viel Freude wie ich an diesem Projektbuch und zeigst mir deine Entwürfe in den sozialen Medien mit dem Hashtag #designdeinklimperklein!

Liebste Grüße,
Deine

Pauline

SO WIRD'S GEMACHT

SUPERCOOL

120

Basicshirt

Farben ausprobieren

Entworfen am 1.7.2018

Genäht am 5.7.2018

Genäht für Lotti

Größe 110

klimperklein.

Datum und Größe eintragen

Stoffe einkleben

Eine Seite hat Pauline schon mal ausgefüllt, damit du siehst, was du alles eintragen kannst.

Alle Infos notieren

MASSTABELLEN

Name:

Datum			
Körperhöhe			
Bauchumfang			
Brustumfang			
Beinlänge innen			
Armlänge außen			

Name:

Datum			
Körperhöhe			
Bauchumfang			
Brustumfang			
Beinlänge innen			
Armlänge außen			

Name:

Datum			
Körperhöhe			
Bauchumfang			
Brustumfang			
Beinlänge innen			
Armlänge außen			

Name:

Datum			
Körperhöhe			
Bauchumfang			
Brustumfang			
Beinlänge innen			
Armlänge außen			

Name:

Datum			
Körperhöhe			
Bauchumfang			
Brustumfang			
Beinlänge innen			
Armlänge außen			

Name:

Datum			
Körperhöhe			
Bauchumfang			
Brustumfang			
Beinlänge innen			
Armlänge außen			

Name:

Datum			
Körperhöhe			
Bauchumfang			
Brustumfang			
Beinlänge innen			
Armlänge außen			

Name:

Datum			
Körperhöhe			
Bauchumfang			
Brustumfang			
Beinlänge innen			
Armlänge außen			

MEIN NÄHPLANER

Saison			
Größe			

Saison			
Größe			

Saison			
Größe			

Saison			
Größe			

Saison			
Größe			

Saison			
Größe			

Saison			
Größe			

Saison			
Größe			

Die folgende Maßtabelle bezieht sich auf die Körpermaße des Kindes. Die Zeichnung zeigt, wo gemessen wird. Bei den angegebenen Körpermaßen sitzt das fertige Kleidungsstück in Länge und Weite so, wie vorgesehen. Damit das Teil auch den eigenen Vorstellungen entspricht, vergleicht man am besten ein gut passendes Kleidungsstück direkt mit dem Schnittmuster. So geht man auf Nummer sicher.
Für sehr schmale oder sehr kräftige Kinder ist es immer eine gute Lösung, verschiedene Größen für Länge und Weite zu wählen.
Für besonders schmale Kinder oder einen körpernahen Sitz wird die Kleidergröße gewählt, die der gewünschten Weite entspricht, und die Säume von Ärmeln, Beinen und Körper auf die der Körpergröße entsprechende Kleidergröße verlängert.
Für kräftige Kinder oder einen lässigen Sitz wird die Kleidergröße ebenfalls nach gewünschter Weite ausgesucht und im Anschluss auf die zur Körpergröße passende Länge eingekürzt.

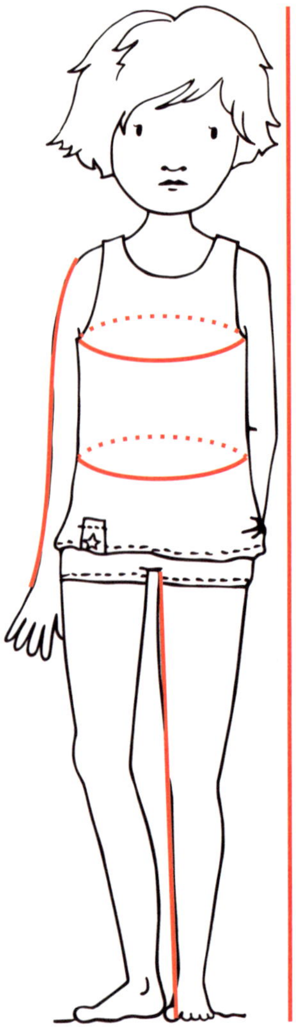

Körpergröße in cm*	104	110	116	122	128	134	140	146	152	158	164
Bauchumfang	50	52	54	56	58	60	62	64	66	68	70
Brustumfang	54	56	58	60	62	64	66	68	70	72	74
Beininnenlänge	38	43	48	53	56	60	64	67	70	73	76
Armlänge außen	33	35	37	40	42	44	47	49	52	54	61

* entspricht Kleidergröße

MODELLE

Die Nähanleitungen und Schnittmuster der Projekte findest Du in diesen beiden Büchern von Pauline Dohmen:

TOPP 6402
ISBN 978-3-7724-6402-7

20	TRENDSETTER	Bündchenmütze
24	HOT & COLD	Beanie und Schal
44	A STAR IS BORN	Raglanshirt lang, mit Motiv
48	TRENDSETTER	Raglanshirt lang
60	FÜR ALLE FÄLLE	Raglanshirt kurz
114	SUPER BEQUEM	Sweatjacke
150	MÄDCHENTRAUM	Geraffter Rock

TOPP 6482
ISBN 978-3-7724-6482-9

Bündchenmütze

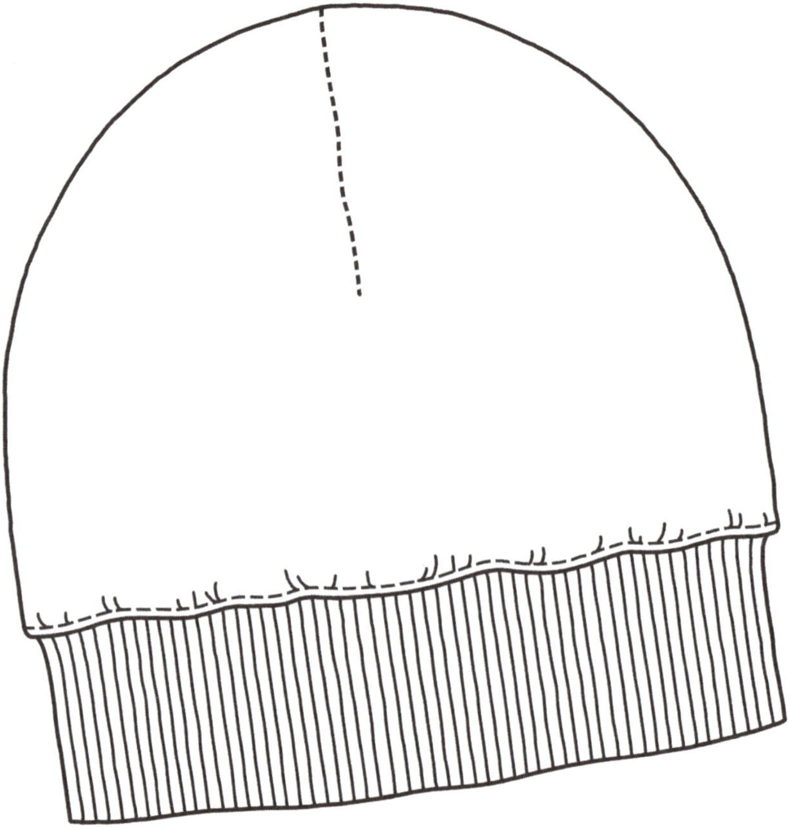

Entworfen am ________________________ Größe

Genäht am ________________________

Genäht für ________________________ ________

Meine Stoffe

Meine Stoffe

Meine Stoffe

Notizen

KUNTERBUNT

Bündchenmütze

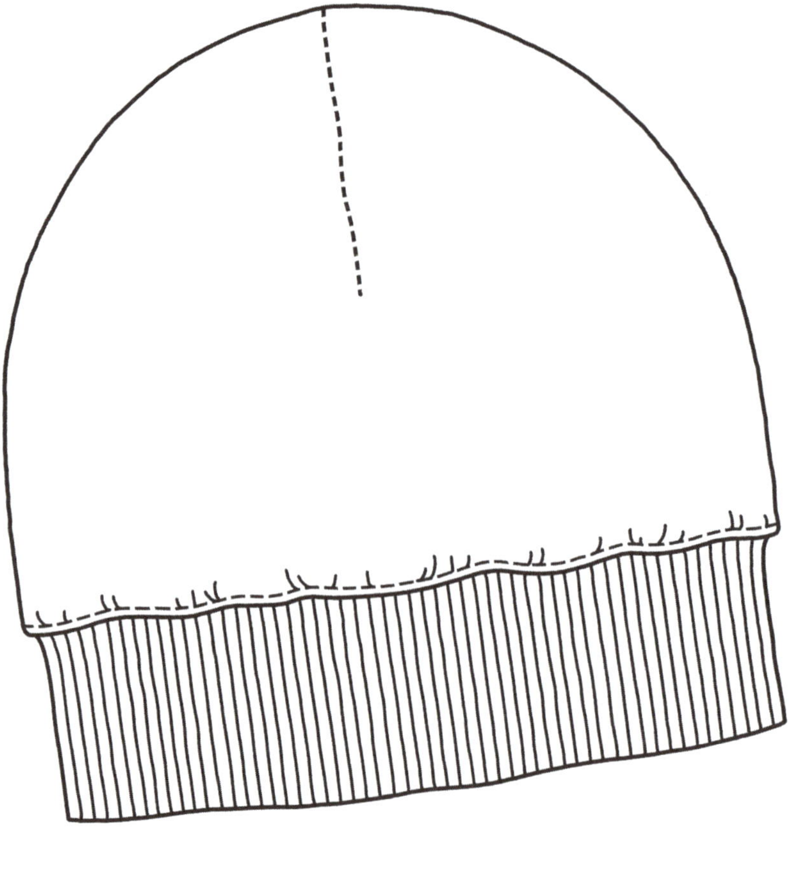

Entworfen am ______________________ Größe

Genäht am ______________________

Genäht für ______________________ ________

Meine Stoffe

Meine Stoffe

Notizen

Meine Stoffe

HOT & COLD

Beanie und Schal

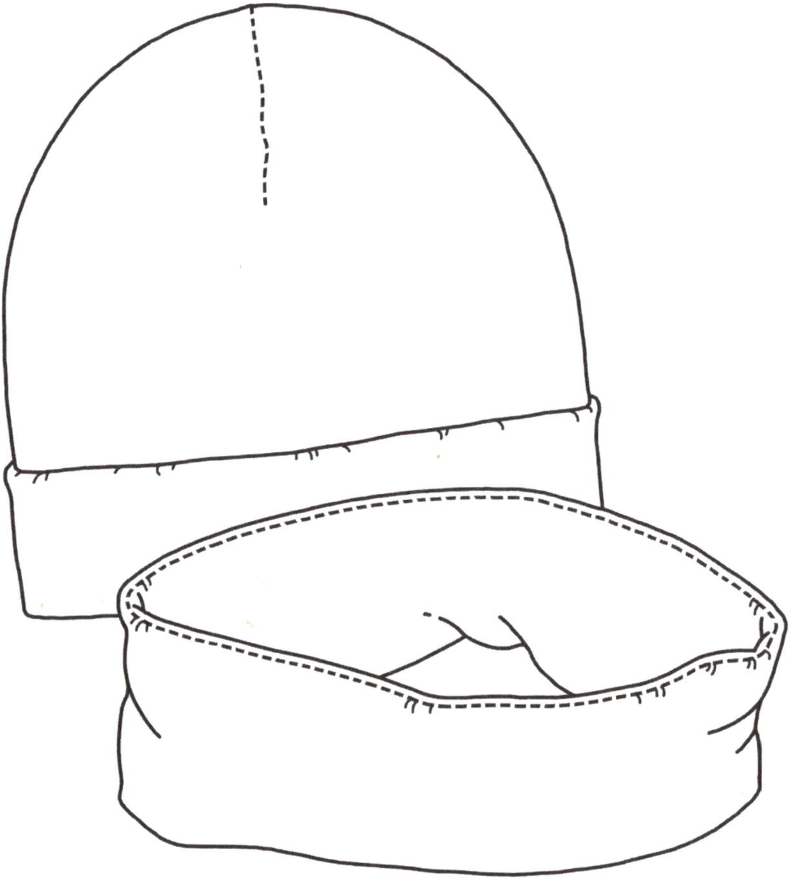

klimperklein.

Entworfen am ______________________ Größe

Genäht am ______________________

Genäht für ______________________ ________

Meine Stoffe

Notizen

Meine Stoffe

Meine Stoffe

HOT & COLD

Beanie und Schal

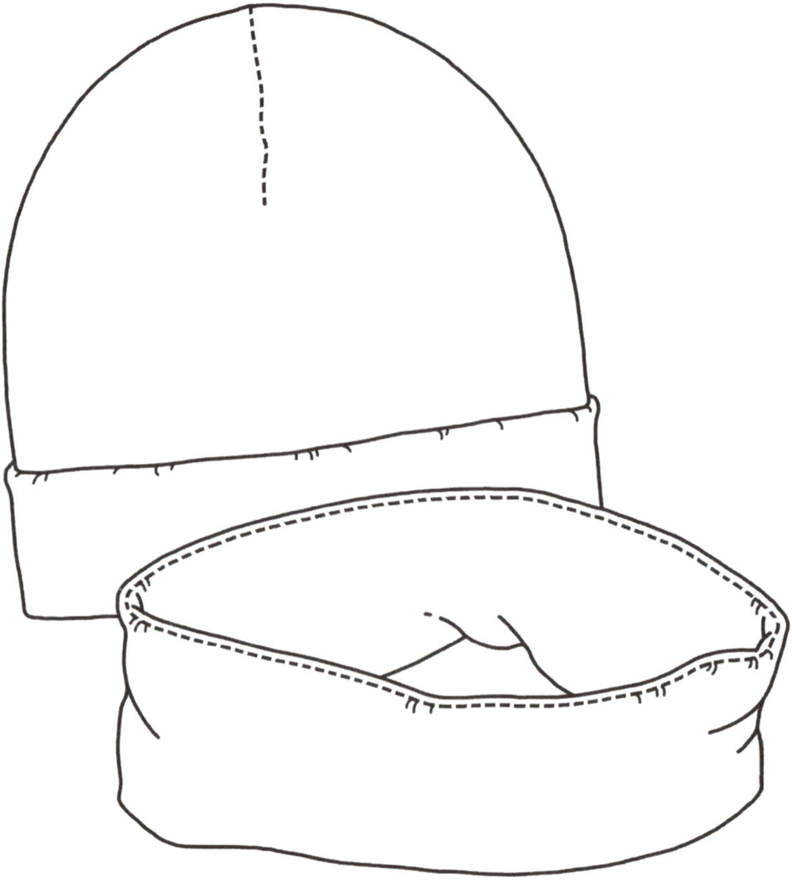

Entworfen am ________________________ Größe

Genäht am ________________________

Genäht für ________________________ ________

Meine Stoffe

Notizen

Meine Stoffe

Meine Stoffe

Meine Stoffe

Meine Stoffe

Meine Stoffe

Notizen

LADIES ONLY

Wäscheset Mädchen

Entworfen am ________________________ Größe

Genäht am ________________________

Genäht für ________________________ ________

LADIES ONLY

Wäscheset Mädchen

Entworfen am ______________________ Größe

Genäht am ______________________

Genäht für ______________________ ________

Meine Stoffe

Meine Stoffe

Notizen

Meine Stoffe

LADIES ONLY

Wäscheset Mädchen

Entworfen am ________________________ Größe

Genäht am ________________________

Genäht für ________________________ ________

Meine Stoffe

Notizen

Meine Stoffe

Meine Stoffe

LADIES ONLY

Wäscheset Mädchen

Entworfen am ________________ Größe

Genäht am ________________

Genäht für ________________ ________

Meine Stoffe

Notizen

Meine Stoffe

Meine Stoffe

BOYS ONLY

Wäscheset Jungs

klimper klein.

Entworfen am ______________________ Größe

Genäht am ______________________

Genäht für ______________________ ________

Meine Stoffe

Meine Stoffe

Meine Stoffe

Notizen

BOYS ONLY

Wäscheset Jungs

Entworfen am ____________________ Größe

Genäht am ____________________

Genäht für ____________________ ________

Meine Stoffe

Meine Stoffe

Notizen

Meine Stoffe

Boys ONLY

Wäscheset Jungs

Entworfen am ______________________ Größe

Genäht am ______________________

Genäht für ______________________ ________

Meine Stoffe

Notizen

Meine Stoffe

Meine Stoffe

BOYS ONLY

Wäscheset Jungs

klimper klein.

Entworfen am ______________________ Größe

Genäht am ______________________

Genäht für ______________________ ________

Meine Stoffe

Notizen

Meine Stoffe

Meine Stoffe

A STAR IS BORN

Raglanshirt lang, mit Motiv

Entworfen am ______________________ Größe

Genäht am ______________________

Genäht für ______________________ ________

Meine Stoffe

Meine Stoffe

Meine Stoffe

Notizen

A STAR IS BORN

Raglanshirt lang, mit Motiv

Entworfen am ______________________ Größe

Genäht am ______________________

Genäht für ______________________ ________

Meine Stoffe

Meine Stoffe

Notizen

Meine Stoffe

Raglanshirt lang

Entworfen am ______________________ Größe

Genäht am ______________________

Genäht für ______________________ ________

Meine Stoffe

Notizen

Meine Stoffe

Meine Stoffe

TRENDSETTER

Raglanshirt lang

Entworfen am ______________________ Größe

Genäht am ______________________

Genäht für ______________________ ________

Meine Stoffe

Notizen

Meine Stoffe

Meine Stoffe

TRENDSETTER

Raglanshirt lang

Entworfen am ________________________ Größe

Genäht am ________________________

Genäht für ________________________ ________

Meine Stoffe

Meine Stoffe

Meine Stoffe

Notizen

TRENDSETTER

Raglanshirt lang

Entworfen am ______________________ Größe

Genäht am ______________________

Genäht für ______________________ ________

Meine Stoffe

Meine Stoffe

Notizen

Meine Stoffe

TRENDSETTER

Raglanshirt lang

Entworfen am ________________________ Größe

Genäht am ________________________

Genäht für ________________________ ________

Meine Stoffe

Notizen

Meine Stoffe

Meine Stoffe

TRENDSETTER

Raglanshirt lang

klimperklein.

Entworfen am ______________________ Größe

Genäht am ______________________

Genäht für ______________________ ________

Meine Stoffe

Notizen

Meine Stoffe

Meine Stoffe

FÜR ALLE FÄLLE

Raglanshirt kurz

Entworfen am ________________________ Größe

Genäht am ________________________

Genäht für ________________________ ________

Meine Stoffe

Meine Stoffe

Meine Stoffe

Notizen

Raglanshirt kurz

Entworfen am ________________________ Größe

Genäht am ________________________

Genäht für ________________________ ________

Meine Stoffe

Meine Stoffe

Notizen

Meine Stoffe

Raglanshirt kurz

Entworfen am ________________________ Größe

Genäht am ________________________

Genäht für ________________________ ________

Meine Stoffe

Notizen

Meine Stoffe

Meine Stoffe

FÜR ALLE FÄLLE

Raglanshirt kurz

Entworfen am ________________________ Größe

Genäht am ________________________

Genäht für ________________________ ________

Meine Stoffe

Notizen

Meine Stoffe

Meine Stoffe

FÜR ALLE FÄLLE

Raglanshirt kurz

Entworfen am ______________________ Größe

Genäht am ______________________

Genäht für ______________________ ________

Meine Stoffe

Meine Stoffe

Meine Stoffe

Notizen

Raglanshirt kurz

Entworfen am ______________________ Größe

Genäht am ______________________

Genäht für ______________________ ________

Meine Stoffe

Meine Stoffe

Notizen

Meine Stoffe

GANZ IM TREND

Simples Shirt mit Motiv

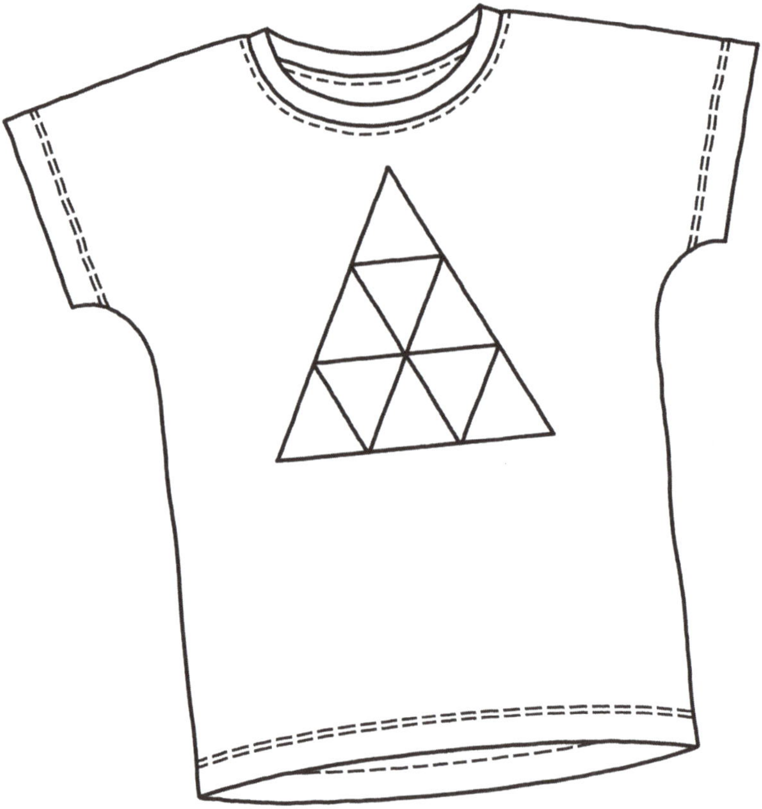

Entworfen am ________________________ Größe

Genäht am ________________________

Genäht für ________________________ ________

Meine Stoffe

Notizen

Meine Stoffe

Meine Stoffe

GANZ IM TREND

Simples Shirt mit Motiv

Entworfen am ______________________ Größe

Genäht am ______________________

Genäht für ______________________ ________

Meine Stoffe

Notizen

Meine Stoffe

Meine Stoffe

TOP AKTUELL

Simples Shirt

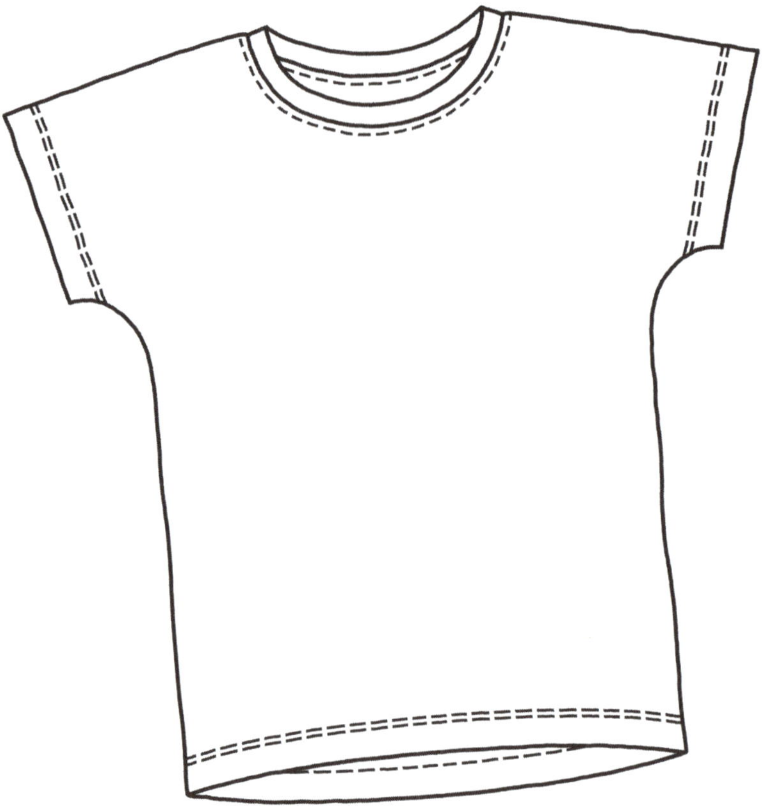

Entworfen am ______________________ Größe

Genäht am ______________________

Genäht für ______________________ ________

Meine Stoffe

Meine Stoffe

Meine Stoffe

Notizen

TOP AKTUELL

Simples Shirt

Entworfen am ______________________ Größe

Genäht am ______________________

Genäht für ______________________ ________

Meine Stoffe

Meine Stoffe

Notizen

Meine Stoffe

Simples Shirt

Entworfen am ______________________ Größe

Genäht am ______________________

Genäht für ______________________ ________

Meine Stoffe

Notizen

Meine Stoffe

Meine Stoffe

Meine Stoffe

Notizen

Meine Stoffe

Meine Stoffe

HOT SUMMER

T-Shirt, kurzarm

Entworfen am ______________________ Größe

Genäht am ______________________

Genäht für ______________________ ________

HOT SUMMER

T-Shirt, kurzarm

Entworfen am ____________________ Größe

Genäht am ____________________

Genäht für ____________________ ________

Meine Stoffe

Meine Stoffe

Meine Stoffe

Notizen

HOT SUMMER

T-Shirt, kurzarm

Entworfen am ______________________ Größe

Genäht am ______________________

Genäht für ______________________ ________

Meine Stoffe

Meine Stoffe

Notizen

Meine Stoffe

HOT SUMMER

T-Shirt, kurzarm

Entworfen am ________________________ Größe

Genäht am ________________________

Genäht für ________________________ ________

Meine Stoffe

Notizen

Meine Stoffe

Meine Stoffe

T-Shirt, kurzarm

Entworfen am ________________________ Größe

Genäht am ________________________

Genäht für ________________________ ________

Meine Stoffe

Notizen

Meine Stoffe

Meine Stoffe

HOT SUMMER

T-Shirt, kurzarm

Entworfen am ______________________ Größe

Genäht am ______________________

Genäht für ______________________ ________

Meine Stoffe

Meine Stoffe

Meine Stoffe

Notizen

Basicshirt, langarm

Entworfen am ______________________ Größe

Genäht am ______________________

Genäht für ______________________ ________

Meine Stoffe

Meine Stoffe

Notizen

Meine Stoffe

MACHT ALLES MIT

Basicshirt, langarm

Entworfen am ________________________ Größe

Genäht am ________________________

Genäht für ________________________ ________

Meine Stoffe

Notizen

Meine Stoffe

Meine Stoffe

Basicshirt, langarm

Entworfen am ________________________ Größe

Genäht am ________________________

Genäht für ________________________ ________

Notizen

Meine Stoffe

Meine Stoffe

Meine Stoffe

MACHT ALLES MIT

Basicshirt, langarm

Entworfen am ________________________ Größe

Genäht am ________________________

Genäht für ________________________ ________

Meine Stoffe

Meine Stoffe

Meine Stoffe

Notizen

MACHT ALLES MIT

Basicshirt, langarm

Entworfen am ________________________ Größe

Genäht am ________________________

Genäht für ________________________ ________

Meine Stoffe

Meine Stoffe

Notizen

Meine Stoffe

Meine Stoffe

Notizen

Meine Stoffe

Meine Stoffe

LIEBLINGSSTÜCK

Mädchenshirt

Entworfen am ________________________ Größe

Genäht am ________________________

Genäht für ________________________ ________

klimperklein.

LIEBLINGSSTÜCK

Mädchenshirt

Entworfen am ______________________ Größe

Genäht am ______________________

Genäht für ______________________ ________

Meine Stoffe

Notizen

Meine Stoffe

Meine Stoffe

LIEBLINGSSTÜCK

Mädchenshirt

Entworfen am ______________________ Größe

Genäht am ______________________

Genäht für ______________________ ________

Meine Stoffe

Meine Stoffe

Meine Stoffe

Notizen

LIEBLINGSSTÜCK

Mädchenshirt

Entworfen am ______________________ Größe

Genäht am ______________________

Genäht für ______________________ ________

Meine Stoffe

Meine Stoffe

Notizen

Meine Stoffe

LIEBLINGSSTÜCK

Mädchenshirt

Entworfen am ________________________ Größe

Genäht am ________________________

Genäht für ________________________ ________

Meine Stoffe

Notizen

Meine Stoffe

Meine Stoffe

Meine Stoffe

Notizen

Meine Stoffe

Meine Stoffe

SUPER BEQUEM

Sweatjacke

Entworfen am ________________________ Größe

Genäht am ________________________

Genäht für ________________________ ________

SUPER BEQUEM

Sweatjacke

Entworfen am ______________________ Größe

Genäht am ______________________

Genäht für ______________________ ________

Meine Stoffe

Meine Stoffe

Meine Stoffe

Notizen

SUPER BEQUEM

Sweatjacke

Entworfen am ______________________ Größe

Genäht am ______________________

Genäht für ______________________ ________

Meine Stoffe

Meine Stoffe

Notizen

Meine Stoffe

MOLLIG WARM

Hoodie mit Wickelkapuze und Motiv

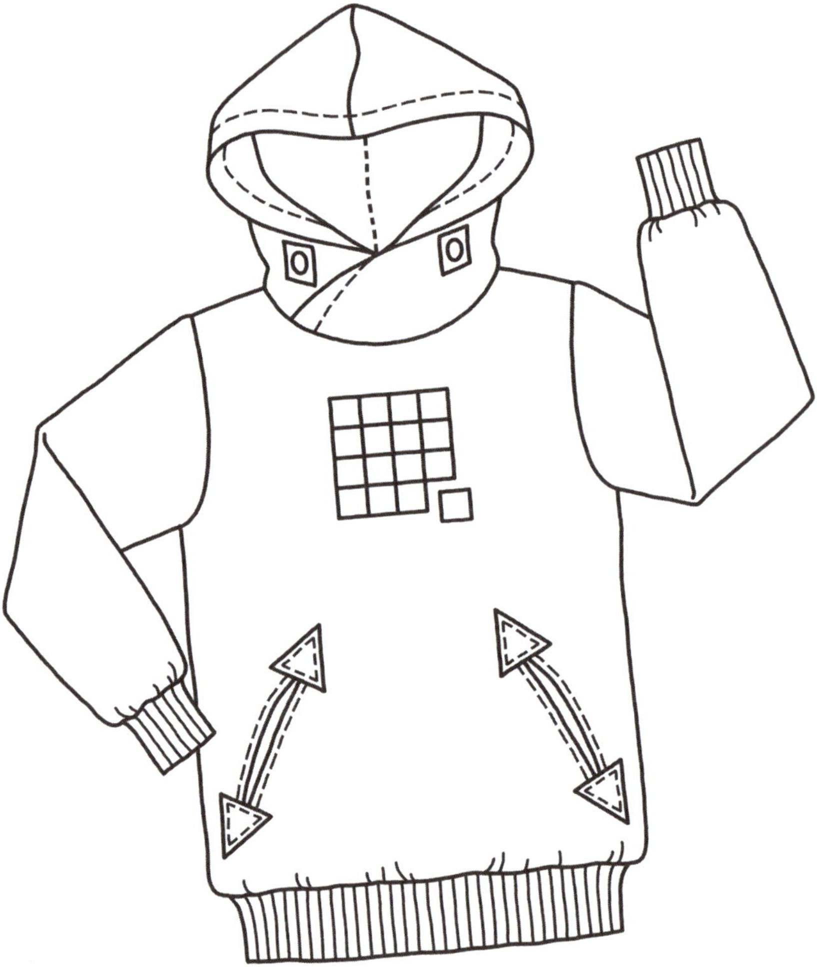

Entworfen am ______________________ Größe

Genäht am ______________________

Genäht für ______________________ ________

Meine Stoffe

Notizen

Meine Stoffe

Meine Stoffe

Meine Stoffe

Meine Stoffe

Meine Stoffe

Notizen

OUTDOOR-TREND

Hoodie mit Wickelkapuze

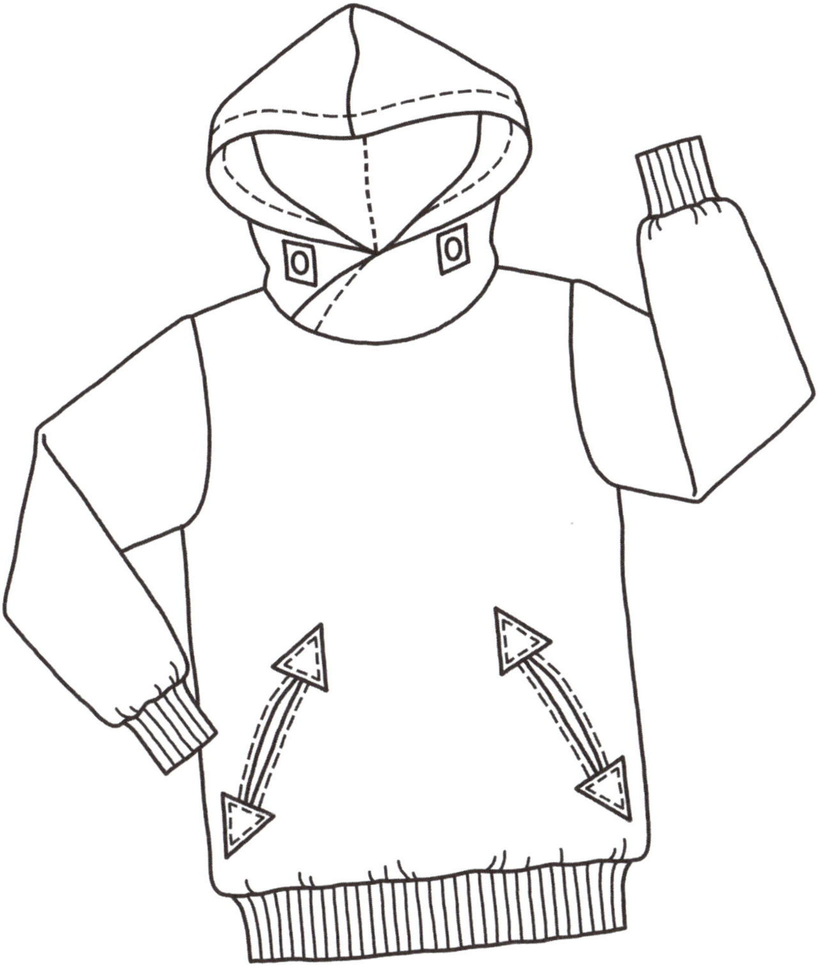

Entworfen am ________________________ Größe

Genäht am ________________________

Genäht für ________________________ _________

OUTDOOR-TREND

Hoodie mit Wickelkapuze

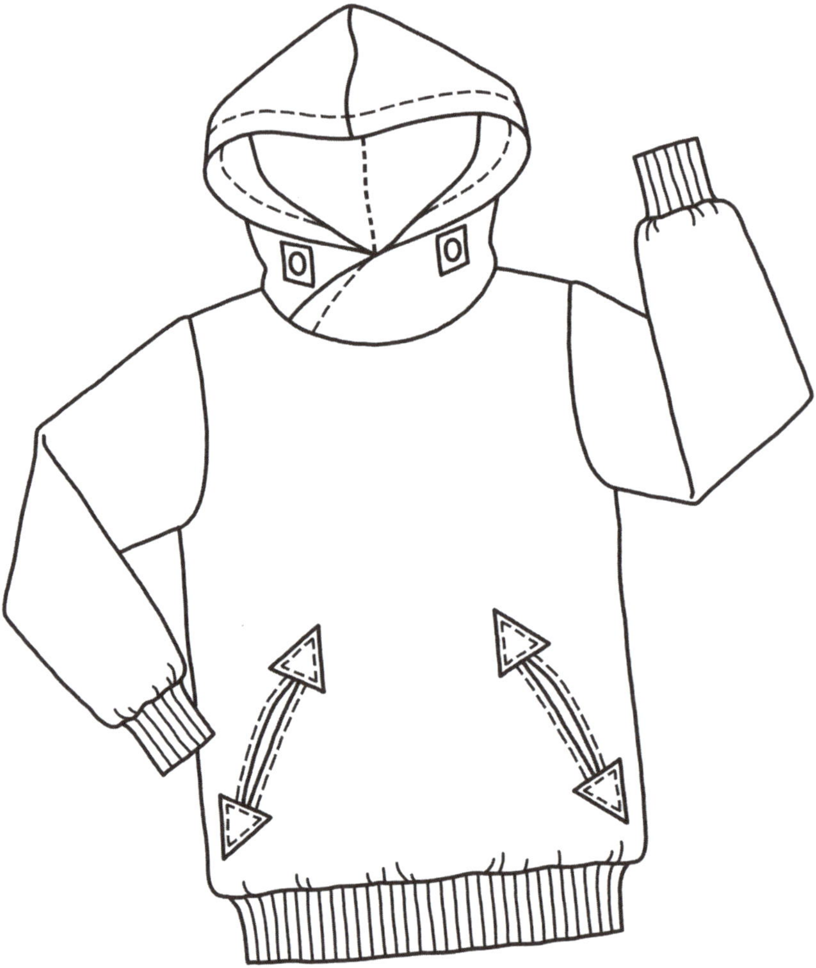

Entworfen am ______________________ Größe

Genäht am ______________________

Genäht für ______________________ ________

Meine Stoffe

Notizen

Meine Stoffe

Meine Stoffe

SUPERLÄSSIG

Hoodie mit Astronautenkapuze

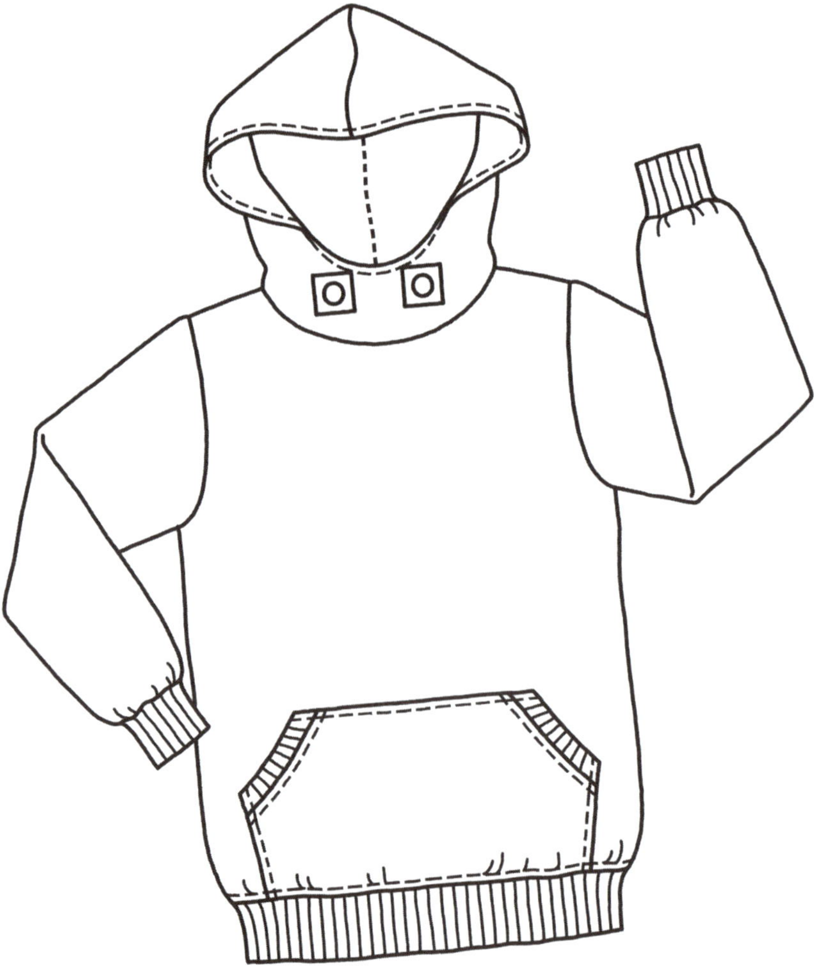

Entworfen am ______________________ Größe

Genäht am ______________________

Genäht für ______________________ ________

Meine Stoffe

Notizen

Meine Stoffe

Meine Stoffe

SUPERLÄSSIG

Hoodie mit Astronautenkapuze

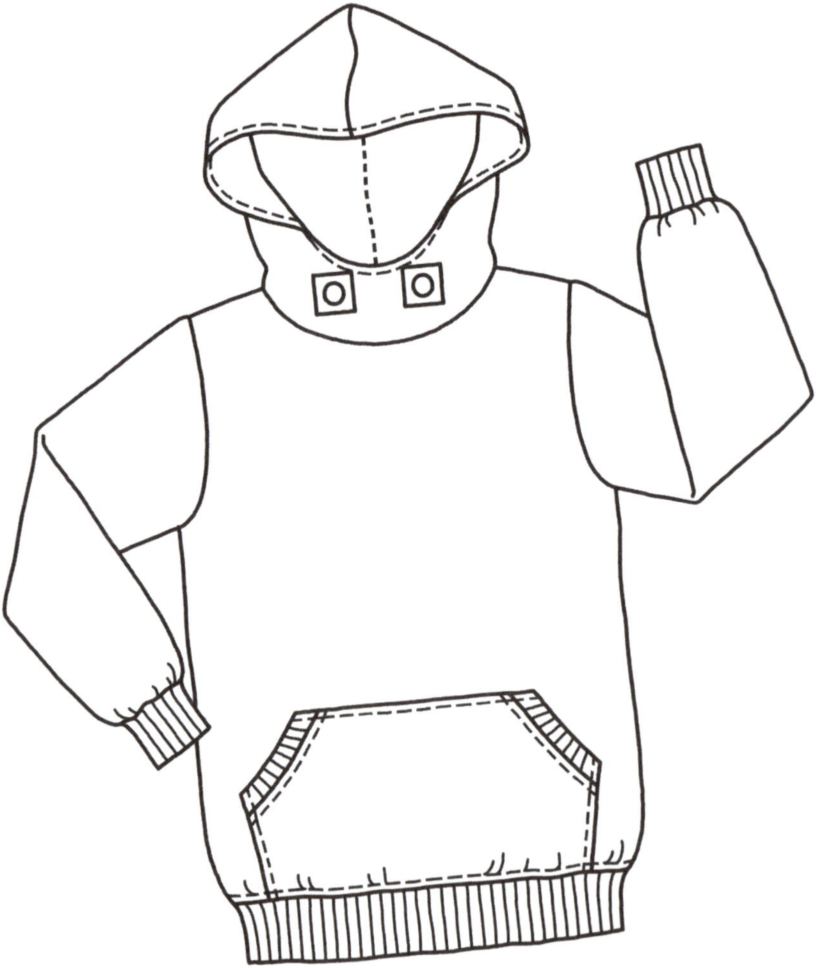

Entworfen am ________________________ Größe

Genäht am ________________________

Genäht für ________________________ ________

Meine Stoffe

Meine Stoffe

Meine Stoffe

Notizen

Meine Stoffe

Meine Stoffe

Notizen

Meine Stoffe

Hoodiekleid

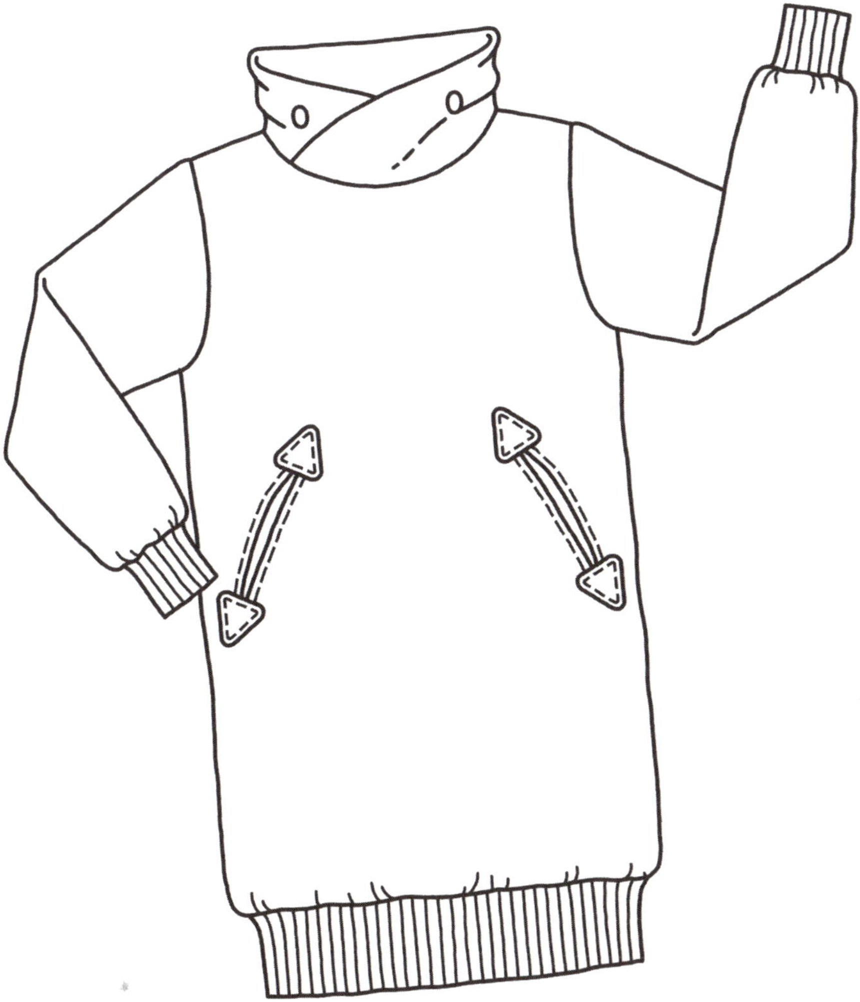

Entworfen am ____________________ Größe

Genäht am ____________________

Genäht für ____________________ ________

EINFACH BEQUEM

Hoodiekleid

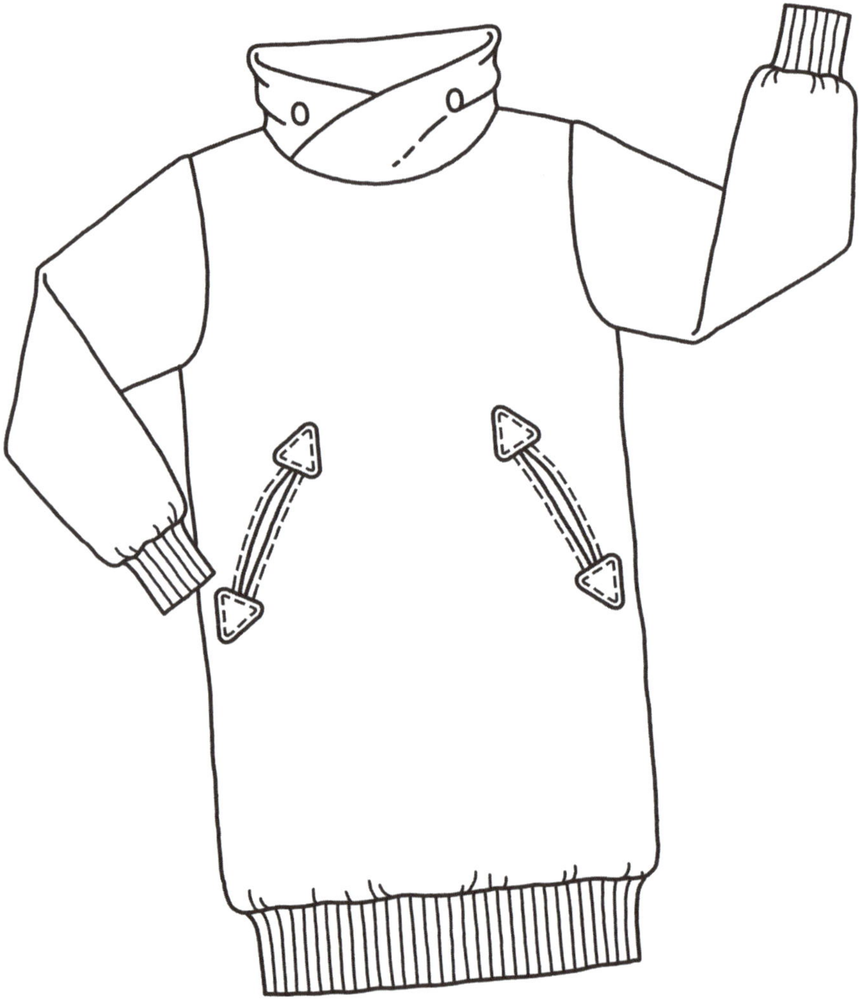

Entworfen am ______________________ Größe

Genäht am ______________________

Genäht für ______________________ ________

Meine Stoffe

Notizen

Meine Stoffe

Meine Stoffe

EINFACH BEQUEM

Hoodiekleid

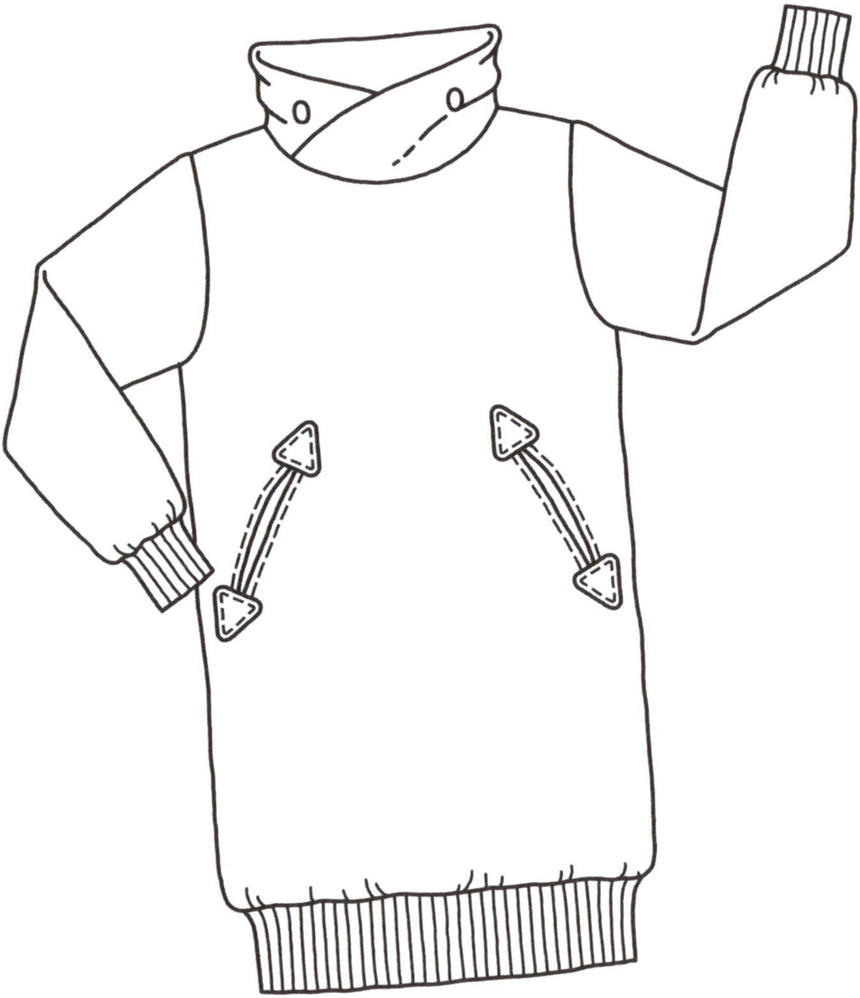

Entworfen am ________________________ Größe

Genäht am ________________________

Genäht für ________________________ ________

Meine Stoffe

Meine Stoffe

Notizen

Meine Stoffe

ZUM KOMBINIEREN

Skaterrock

Entworfen am ______________________ Größe

Genäht am ______________________

Genäht für ______________________ ________

Meine Stoffe

Meine Stoffe

Meine Stoffe

Notizen

ZUM KOMBINIEREN

Skaterrock

Entworfen am ______________________ Größe

Genäht am ______________________

Genäht für ______________________ ________

Meine Stoffe

Meine Stoffe

Notizen

Meine Stoffe

ZUM KOMBINIEREN

Skaterrock

Entworfen am ______________________ Größe

Genäht am ______________________

Genäht für ______________________ ________

Meine Stoffe

Notizen

Meine Stoffe

Meine Stoffe

GUT GELAUNT

Skaterkleid

Entworfen am ____________________ Größe

Genäht am ____________________

Genäht für ____________________ ________

Notizen

Meine Stoffe

Meine Stoffe

Meine Stoffe

GUT GELAUNT

Skaterkleid

Entworfen am ______________________ Größe

Genäht am ______________________

Genäht für ______________________ ________

Meine Stoffe

Meine Stoffe

Meine Stoffe

Notizen

GUT GELAUNT

Skaterkleid

Entworfen am ______________________ Größe

Genäht am ______________________

Genäht für ______________________ ________

Meine Stoffe

Meine Stoffe

Notizen

Meine Stoffe

Meine Stoffe

Notizen

Meine Stoffe

Meine Stoffe

Geraffter Rock

Entworfen am ________________________ Größe

Genäht am ________________________

Genäht für ________________________ ________

klimperklein.

Geraffter Rock

Entworfen am ______________________ Größe

Genäht am ______________________

Genäht für ______________________ ________

Meine Stoffe

Notizen

Meine Stoffe

Meine Stoffe

CHILL OUT

Jogginghose

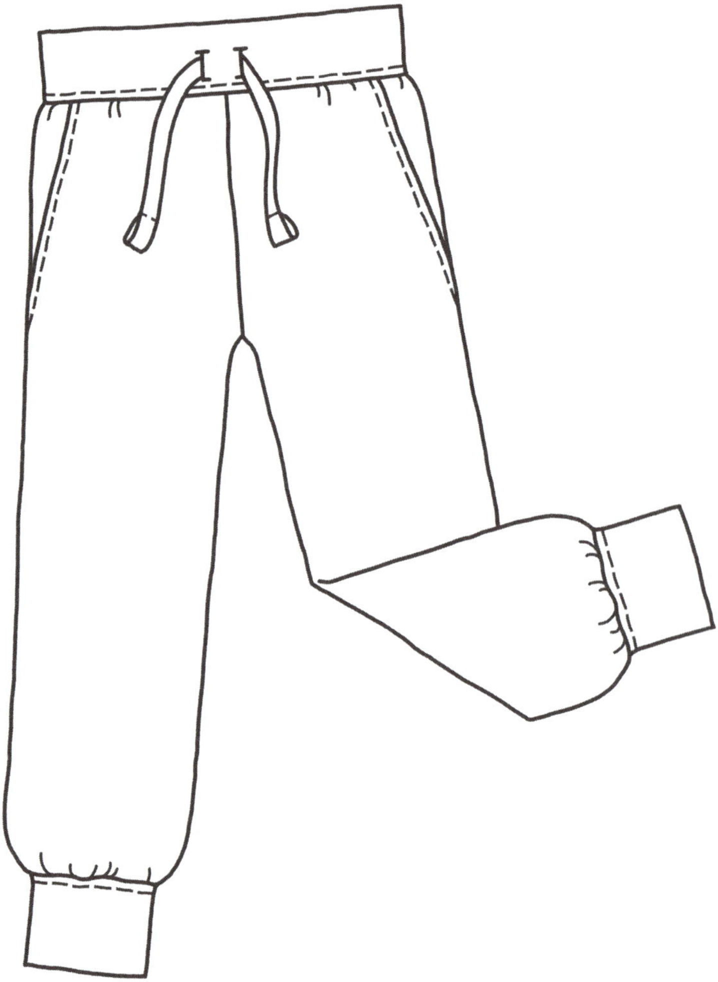

Entworfen am ______________________ Größe

Genäht am ______________________

Genäht für ______________________ ________

Meine Stoffe

Meine Stoffe

Meine Stoffe

Notizen

CHILL OUT

Jogginghose

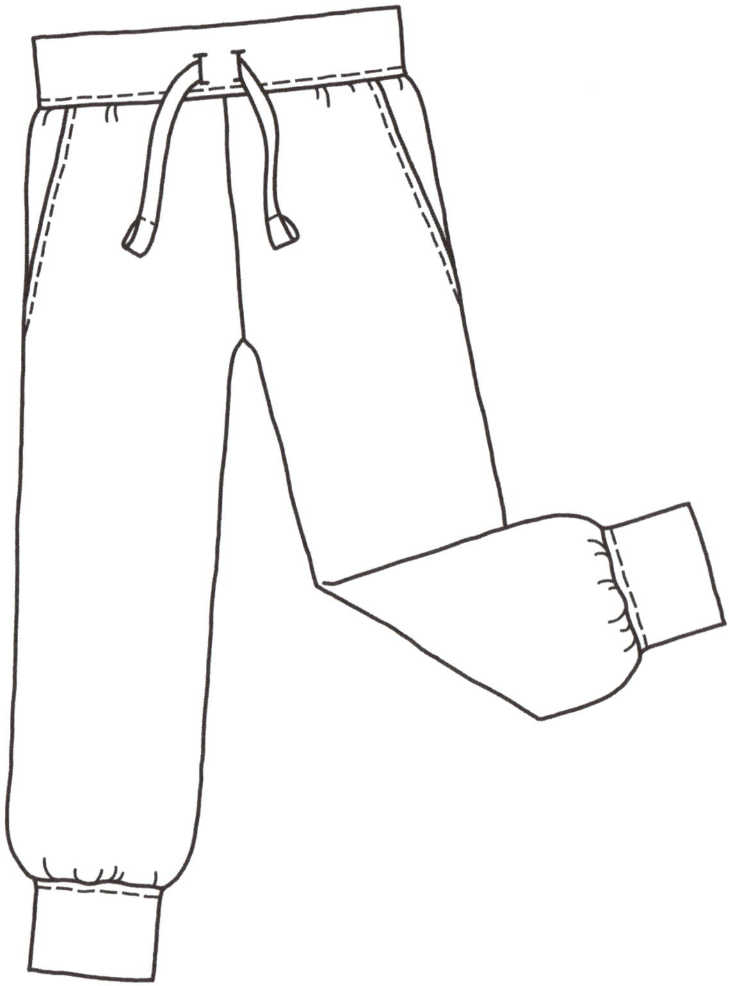

Entworfen am ________________________ Größe

Genäht am ________________________

Genäht für ________________________ ________

Meine Stoffe

Meine Stoffe

Notizen

Meine Stoffe

CHILL OUT

Jogginghose

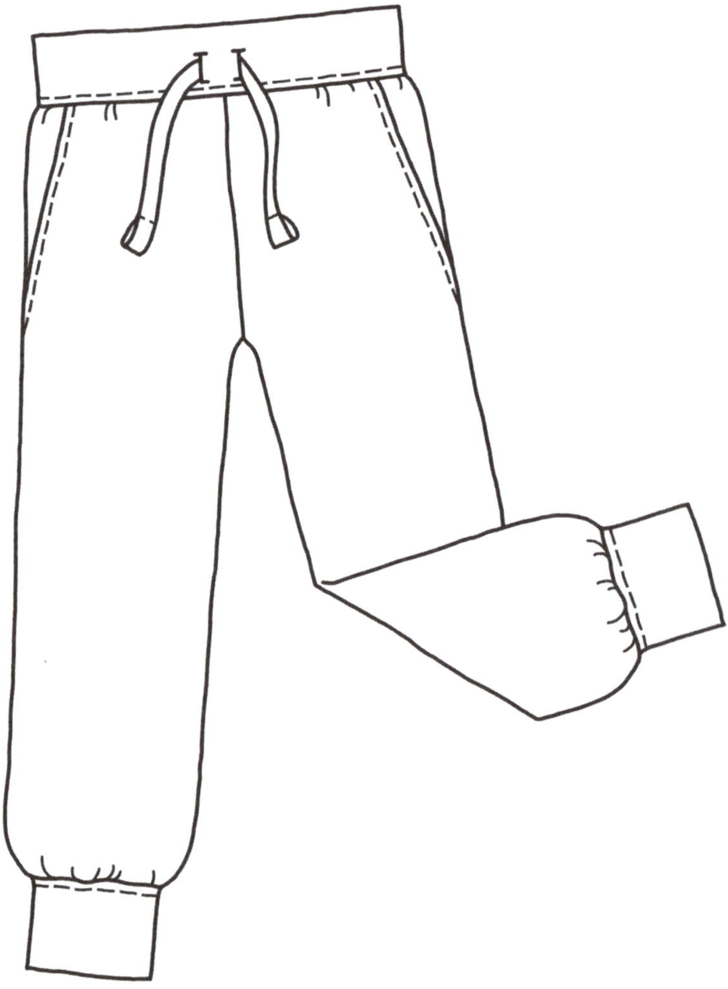

Entworfen am ______________________ Größe

Genäht am ______________________

Genäht für ______________________ __________

Meine Stoffe

Notizen

Meine Stoffe

Meine Stoffe

Pauline Dohmen lebt mit ihren fünf Kindern in Göttingen. Schon von Kindheitstagen an handarbeits- und nähverrückt, geriet sie nach einem ausgedehnten Ausflug in die Medizin während ihrer zweiten Elternzeit in die kunsthandwerkliche Selbstständigkeit und lebt seit 2011 unter dem Label Klimperklein ihren Traum, mit eigenen Schnittideen samt ausführlichen Anleitungen auch andere zu begeistern. Funktionalität, gute Passform und schlichte Schnittführung mit viel Platz für eigene Kreativität stehen dabei im Vordergrund.

Über den Weg zur perfekten Ausstattung für die ganze Familie bloggt sie unter www.klimperklein.de.

Pauline Dohmen im Video: topp-kreativ.de/jersey

Hilfestellung zu allen Fragen, die Materialien und Kreativbücher betreffen: Frau Erika Noll berät Sie. Rufen Sie an: 05052/911858*

*normale Telefongebühren

PRODUKTMANAGEMENT: Eva-Barbara Zirn

ZEICHNUNGEN: Ursula Schwab, Haselund (alle übrigen)

FIGURINE (S. 16): Angela Pickard, Sundern

LAYOUT: Petra Theilfarth

DRUCK UND BINDUNG: DRUK-INTRO S.A., Polen

1. Auflage 2018

ISBN 978-3-7724-8152-9 • Best.-Nr. 8152